DINOSAURS
OF THE UPPER TRIASSIC
& THE LOWER JURASSIC

D AVID & O LIVER W EST

F IREFLY B OOKS

A FIREFLY BOOK

Published by Firefly Books Ltd. 2016

First printing

Publisher Cataloging-in-Publication Data (U.S.)

Names: West, David, 1956-, author.
Title: Dinosaurs of the Upper Triassic & Lower Jurassic : 25 dinosaurs / David West.
Description: Richmond Hill, Ontario, Canada : Firefly Books, 2016. | Series: Dinosaurs. | Includes
    index. | Summary: "An illustrated guide of 25 of the best-known dinosaurs of the period,
    providing up-to-date information with highly detailed computer generated artwork. Illustrated
    introductory spreads provide background information on the time periods in which the
    dinosaurs lived" -- Provided by publisher.
Identifiers: ISBN 978-1-77085-841-1 (paperback) | 978-1-77085-842-8 (hardcover)
Subjects: LCSH: Dinosaurs – Juvenile literature.
Classification: LCC QE861.5W478 |DDC 567.9 – dc23

Library and Archives Canada Cataloguing in Publication

West, David, 1956-, author
        Dinosaurs of the upper Triassic & lower Jurassic : 25 dinos... / David West.
(Dinosaurs)
Includes index.
ISBN 978-1-77085-842-8 (hardback).--ISBN 978-1-77085-841-1 (paperback)
        1. Dinosaurs--Juvenile literature. 2. Paleontology--Triassic--Juvenile
literature. 3. Paleontology--Jurassic--Juvenile literature. I. Title.
QE861.5.W4695 2016   j567.9   C2016-902148-3

Published in the United States by
Firefly Books (U.S.) Inc.
P.O. Box 1338, Ellicott Station
Buffalo, New York 14205

Published in Canada by
Firefly Books Ltd.
50 Staples Avenue, Unit 1
Richmond Hill, Ontario L4B 0A7

Printed in China

Text by David and Oliver West
Illustrations by David West

Produced by David West
Children's Books,
6 Princeton Court, 55 Felsham
Road, London SW15 1AZ

CONTENTS

The Upper Triassic lasted from approximately 235 to 201 million years ago. Over this long period of time the once-large landmass known as Pangea began to split apart into two main continents, Laurasia and Gondwana. Between them the Tethys Sea was formed. The climate was warm and dry with deserts covering much of the interior. It was during this period that dinosaurs evolved from the **archosaurs** that dominated the landscape, along with **therapsids**. The period ended with the Triassic-Jurassic mass extinction event that wiped out around half of all the animal species.

The following period, the Lower Jurassic, lasted from 201 to 176 million years ago. The dinosaurs had survived the mass extinction event and became the dominant reptiles of the land. **Pterosaurs**, the flying reptiles, ruled the sky while in the oceans marine reptiles, such as the **ichthyosaurs** and the **plesiosaurs**, became the main species.

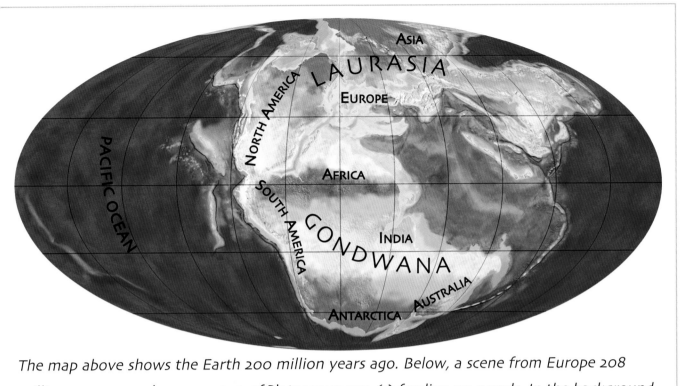

The map above shows the Earth 200 million years ago. Below, a scene from Europe 208 million years ago, shows a group of Plateosauruses (1) feeding on cycads. In the background a lone Liliensternus (2) is hunting for prey. A group of Procompsognathuses (3) run for the safety of the cycads to hide.

AARDONYX

Aardonyx gets it name from the state in which its claws were found, encrusted with mud and earth. The name means "earth claw." *Aardonyx* was a very important find for paleontologists because it confirmed their belief that **sauropodomorphs** evolved from bipedal to quadrupedal herbivores. Although it was still primarily bipedal, *Aardonyx* would quite happily have gone onto all fours to feed and browse for vegetation. *Aardonyx*, like its ancestors and later **sauropods**, had a long neck and tail. Its small head had cheeks that it would fill with vegetation.

Aardonyx lived **200–190 million years ago**. Its fossil remains were found in South Africa. It grew to more than 33 feet (10 m) long and weighed more than 2 tons (1.8 tonnes).

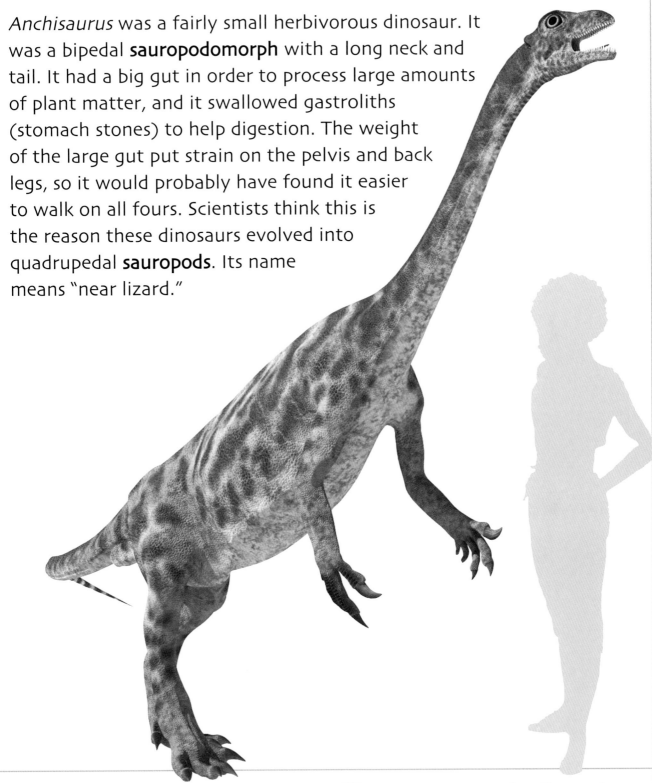

Anchisaurus was a fairly small herbivorous dinosaur. It was a bipedal **sauropodomorph** with a long neck and tail. It had a big gut in order to process large amounts of plant matter, and it swallowed gastroliths (stomach stones) to help digestion. The weight of the large gut put strain on the pelvis and back legs, so it would probably have found it easier to walk on all fours. Scientists think this is the reason these dinosaurs evolved into quadrupedal **sauropods**. Its name means "near lizard."

Anchisaurus lived between **190–174 million years ago**. Its fossil remains were found in South Africa and China, Asia. It grew to a length of around 6.6 feet (2 m) and weighed about 60 pounds (27 kg).

BARAPASAURUS

Barapasaurus was one of the earliest-known **sauropod** dinosaurs. Its name means "big-legged lizard," from "barapa" meaning "big legged" in several Indian languages. It lived during the Lower Jurassic period in what is today India. India was joined to Africa and Antarctica as part of Gondwana during this time. Fossil remains of trees and bones suggest that a herd of *Barapasauruses* were feeding in a woodland when they were washed away in a catastrophic flood.

Barapasaurus lived around **190–170 million years ago**. Fossil remains have been found in India, Asia. It grew to a length of 46 feet (14 m) and weighed in the region of 15 tons (13.6 tonnes).

Coelophysis means "hollow form" after its hollow bones that made it extremely light! It was a small carnivorous **theropod** with a very streamlined and agile build. The hollow bones combined with its long, strong legs meant it could run very quickly to catch small reptiles and mammals. Its long tail provided an excellent balance for high-speed chases. *Coelophysis* had an elongated skull, filled with curved, serrated teeth that were perfect for slicing through flesh. Fossil records show that it may have hunted in packs.

Coelophysis lived between **220–195 million years ago**. Fossil remains have been found in the United States, North America. It grew to 9.8 feet (3 m) in length and weighed between 33 and 44 pounds (15–20 kg).

CRYOLOPHOSAURUS

Its name means "frozen crested lizard" after the fossils, found in Antarctica, showed a fan-shaped crest in front of its eyes. It is the oldest fossil of a meat eater ever found! It was a large carnivorous **theropod** with a slender build. It probably hunted **sauropodomorphs** among the jungles of the continent. Antarctica is a snowy region today but was warm with lush jungles 200 million years ago.

Cryolophosaurus lived between **194–188 million years ago**. Its fossil remains were found in Antarctica. It grew to around 23 feet (7 m) long and weighed about 1,025 pounds (465 kg).

DILOPHOSAURUS

Dilophosaurus was a lightly built, fast-running, carnivorous **theropod** with two large crests that grew from the top of its skull. Its name means "two-crested lizard." Its jaws had a crocodile-like appearance, and some scientists have suggested that they may have lived and hunted in an aquatic environment.

Dilophosaurus lived around **190 million years ago**. Fossil remains have been found in China, Asia, and in the United States, North America. It grew up to 20 feet (6.1 m) long and weighed around 1,102 pounds (500 kg).

EORAPTOR

Its name means "early thief" and it was one of the earliest dinosaurs ever discovered. Although it was named a raptor, it is not related to *Velociraptor* or Dromaeosaurs. In fact, it is believed to be a transitional dinosaur between **theropods** and **sauropodomorphs**. *Eoraptor* was an omnivore, hunting small insects and reptiles, but supplementing its diet with vegetation. It was lightly built, small and agile so that it could escape predators such as *Herrerasaurus* (see page 13), whose fossils were found in the same place.

Eoraptor lived **230–190 million years ago**. Its fossil remains were found in Argentina, South America. It grew to just over 3 feet (1 m) long and weighed about 22 pounds (10 kg).

HERRERASAURUS

Herrerasaurus was named after the rancher who found the first fossils of this dinosaur, and means "Herrera's lizard." It was a very important discovery since it is one of the earliest dinosaurs. It is also one of the earliest-known **theropods**. It had very long legs and ran on its toes, making its strides incredibly long. It had long arms and clawed hands that were perfect for grabbing and holding onto its prey. It had a large head with jaws crammed with sharp, serrated teeth.

Herrerasaurus lived **235–208 million years ago**. Its fossile remains were found in Argentina, South America. It grew to between 9.8 and 19.7 feet (3–6 m) long and weighed in the region of 460 to 770 pounds (210–350 kg).

HETERODONTOSAURUS

Heterodontosaurus means "different-toothed lizard." It had three different types of teeth — incisors for cutting through vegetation, molars for grinding and two small tusks on its lower jaw. It was an **ornithischian** dinosaur, a fleet-footed herbivore. However, its teeth suggest it may have been an omnivore. A distinctive feature of this dinosaur was its hands — it had five fingers, one of which was opposable so it could pick up objects with one hand. It had powerful hind legs with four-toed feet and a long, stiff tail.

Heterodontosaurus lived **205–190 million years ago**. Its fossil remains were found in South Africa. It grew up to 5.7 feet (1.75 m) in length and weighed up to 22 pounds (10 kg).

Jingshanosaurus, meaning "Golden Hill lizard," is named after the village close to where it was found, called Jingshan. It was a large **sauropodomorph**, a bipedal ancestor to *Diplodocus* and *Brachiosaurus*. Its small skull was filled with peg-like teeth for stripping leaves from branches. Like its predecessors, it had a long neck and tail.

Jingshanosaurus lived **199–183 million years ago**. Its fossil remains were found in China, Asia. It grew up to 29.5 feet (9 m) long and weighed about 2 tons (1.8 tonnes).

KOTASAURUS

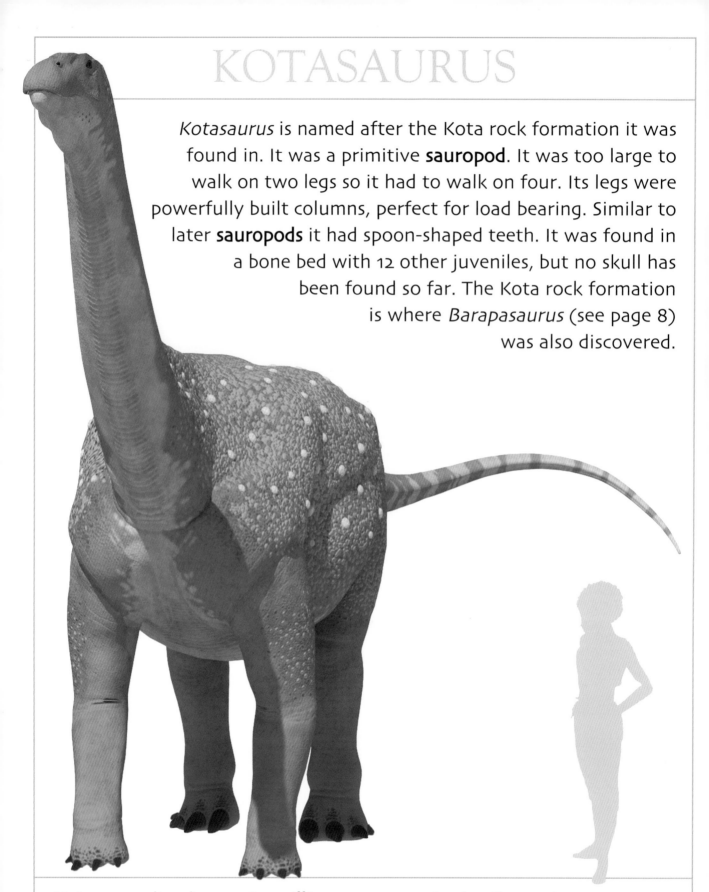

Kotasaurus is named after the Kota rock formation it was found in. It was a primitive **sauropod**. It was too large to walk on two legs so it had to walk on four. Its legs were powerfully built columns, perfect for load bearing. Similar to later **sauropods** it had spoon-shaped teeth. It was found in a bone bed with 12 other juveniles, but no skull has been found so far. The Kota rock formation is where *Barapasaurus* (see page 8) was also discovered.

Kotasaurus lived **205–180 million years ago**. Its fossil remains were found in India, Asia. It grew to 29.5 feet (9 m) long and weighed more than 2.5 tons (2.3 tonnes).

The "lizard from Lesotho" was a small, bipedal plant eater and one of the earliest **ornithischians**. Its long, slim legs and slender tail suggest that it was a fast runner. *Lesothosaurus* had small arms with hands that could not have grasped effectively. Like all **ornithischians** it had a small beak. Behind the beak it had leaf-shaped teeth, and near the front of the upper jaws were 12 fang-like teeth. *Lesothosaurus* could slice up plants but could not chew.

Lesothosaurus lived **199–189 million years ago**. Fossil remains have been found in South Africa. It grew up to 3.3 feet (1 m) long and weighed around 8.8 to 13.2 pounds (4–6 kg).

LEYESAURUS

Leyesaurus, "Leye lizard," is named after the family that found it in the San Juan Province, of Argentina, South America. It is a **sauropodomorph**, a large herbivore that walked on two legs. It had a long neck to access the lush vegetation its smaller cousins could not reach. It is in the same family as *Massospondylus* (see page 22), and shares many of the same features. Its almost complete skull was found along with most of its neck. It had peg-like teeth for raking leaves from branches, and crouched on all fours when browsing low-lying vegetation. Its long tail was a useful counterbalance.

Leyesaurus lived around **199 million years ago**. Its fossil remains were found in Argentina, South America. It grew to 8.2 feet (2.5 m) in length and weighed about 140 pounds (63.5 kg).

Liliensternus was named after the paleontologist, Hugo Rühle von Lilienstern. It was one of the biggest carnivorous **theropods** of its time, and would have hunted dinosaurs as large as *Plateosaurus* (see page 24). It had long, five-fingered hands, strong legs and a double crest along its snout. Its tail was long and stiff, helping it to maintain its balance as it hunted through the woodlands of Europe. It is closely related to *Coelophysis* (see page 9) and *Dilophosaurus* (see page 11).

Liliensternus lived **210–202 million years ago**. Its fossil remains were found in Germany and France, Europe. It grew up to 17.1 feet (5.2 m) long and weighed up to 441 pounds (200 kg).

LOPHOSTROPHEUS

Lophostropheus was a bipedal **theropod** dinosaur of the **coelophysid** family. Its name means "crest vertebrae," after the prominent crests on its neck bones. It is one of the few dinosaurs discovered that may have survived the Triassic–Jurassic mass extinction event (see page 4). Scientists think the crests on its head were used in courtship displays. *Lophostropheus* was a carnivorous hunter and used its powerful legs to run down its prey.

Lophostropheus lived about **200 million years ago**. Fossil remains were found in France, Europe. It grew to a length of 10 feet (3 m) and weighed 220 pounds (99.8 kg).

Lufengosaurus means "Lufeng lizard." It is named after the area in China, Asia, where its fossils were found. It was a very large member of the **massospondylid** family and, like all early **sauropodomorphs**, it had much longer hindlimbs than forelimbs. It probably moved on two legs and on four legs, depending on whether it was running from predators or feeding. It was herbivorous, and its sharp claws and very large thumb claws may have been used for raking foliage from trees — as well as for defense.

Lufengosaurus lived about **190 million years ago**. Fossil remains were found in China. It grew to a length of 30 feet (9.1 m) and had a weight of 1.9 tons (1.7 tonnes).

Massospondylus was a very early herbivorous dinosaur with a long neck and tail. Its head was small with peg-like teeth. Initially it was thought to be a quadruped but now it is believed to be a bipedal herbivorous grazer. Its arms were long with five fingers that were capable of grasping branches when it fed. It belonged to the **sauropodomorph** group. *Massospondylus* was about the size of an elephant, but it was very light due its hollow bones. Its name means "longer vertebrae."

Massospondylus lived between **200–183 million years ago**. Fossils have been found in South Africa, Lesotho and Zimbabwe, Africa. It grew to lengths of 20 feet (6 m) and weighed around 1.5 tons (1.4 tonnes).

Pantydraco means "Panty dragon," after the area where it was found in Wales, Europe, a quarry called Pant-y-ffynnon, and "draco," which means dragon. It was an omnivorous **sauropodomorph**. It had grasping hands with sharp, strong claws. The forelimbs were shorter than the hindlimbs, and the center of gravity was over the pelvis, which suggests a bipedal stance. It probably hunted smaller dinosaurs and insects, and ate plants.

Pantydraco lived between **201–199 million years ago**. Its fossil remains were found in Wales, Europe. It grew to about 9.8 feet (3 m) long and weighed around 110 pounds (50 kg).

PLATEOSAURUS

Plateosaurus means "flat lizard." It was, for its time, a very large bipedal herbivore. It was a **sauropodomorph**, an ancestor of the giant **sauropods** of the Jurassic and Cretaceous periods. Its large, bulky build had a center of gravity over its hips, making walking easier on two legs rather than four. It also had strong frontal arms that could be used to support itself while browsing on low vegetation. It had large claws on its hands that may have been used as protection against predators. **Theropod** teeth have been found among its fossils.

Plateosaurus lived about **210 million years ago**. Fossil remains have been found in Europe, primarily Germany. Its size varied from 14.8 to 32.8 feet (4.5–10 m) long and it weighed up to 4.4 tons (4 tonnes).

Riojasaurus means "La Rioja lizard," after the area where it was found in Argentina, South America. It was a very large quadrupedal herbivore for its time. It was a **sauropodomorph** and an ancestor of the great **sauropods** such as *Diplodocus* and *Brachiosaurus*. It had a bulky build with thick bones and trunk-like legs. Its teeth were spoon-shaped and serrated, ideal for stripping lush leaves from shrubbery and trees.

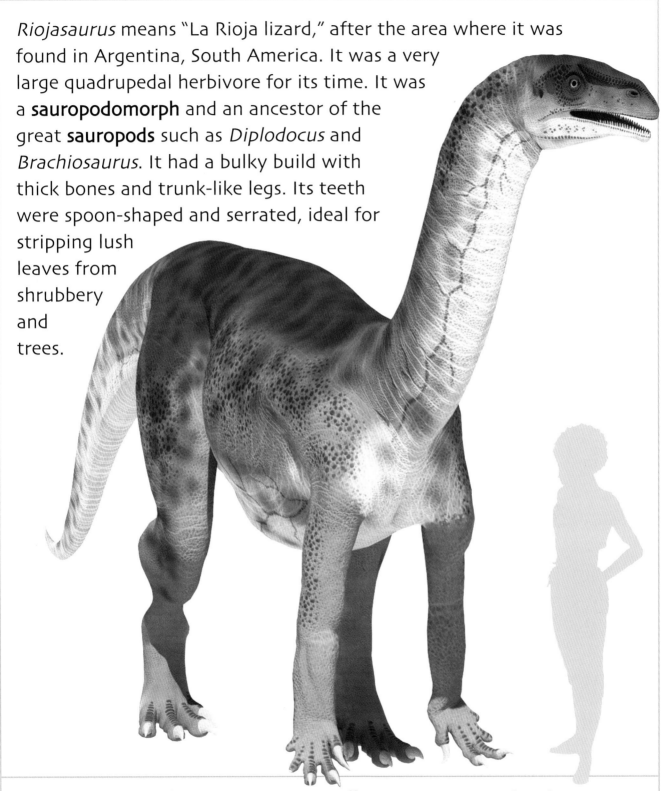

Riojasaurus lived between **220–210 million years ago**. Its fossil remains were found in Argentina, South America. It grew up to 33 feet (10 m) long and weighed 11 tons (10 tonnes).

SALTOPUS

Saltopus means "hopping foot." It was a very early carnivorous reptile known as a **dinosauriform**. Only parts of the skeleton, which did not include the head, have been found. It had hollow bones like modern birds, and most of its length was taken up by its tail. It hunted insects and possibly very small lizards using its petite size and speed to dart around the woodlands and wetlands of Upper Triassic Scotland, Europe.

Saltopus lived between **221–210 million years ago**. Its fossil remains were found in Scotland, Europe. It grew up to about 3.3 feet (1 m) long and weighed no more than 2.2 pounds (1 kg).

Sarcosaurus means "flesh lizard," after its carnivorous diet. It was a **theropod** dinosaur that hunted the plant-eating dinosaurs of the European Jurassic. As only a few parts of its fossilized skeleton have been found, scientists are unsure whether it was a member of the **coelophysaur** family, or a type of early ceratosaur.

Sarcosaurus lived about **194 million years ago**. Its fossil remains were found in England, Europe. It grew up to 11.5 feet (3.5 m) long and weighed about 500 pounds (226.7 kg).

SCUTELLOSAURUS

Scutellosaurus means "little-shielded lizard." It was a herbivorous **ornithischian** dinosaur. It ran around on two legs, but its front limbs were capable of holding its weight while feeding, so it probably would have browsed for food on all fours. It had a small head and a very long tail. *Scutellosaurus'* name comes from the osteoderms covering its back in rows. These gave it protection from predatory dinosaurs such as *Dilophosaurus* (see page 11). It was the ancestor of later armored dinosaurs such as the **ankylosaurs**.

Scutellosaurus lived about **196 million years ago**. Its fossil remains were found in the United States, North America. It grew to about 3.9 feet (1.2 m) long and weighed around 22 pounds (10 kg).

Vulcanodon means "volcano tooth" because its fossils were found between two ancient lava beds. Carnivorous teeth were found around its hips. It was later discovered that these teeth belonged to a **theropod** that was feeding on the carcass before fossilization. *Vulcanodon* was a very early **sauropod** that walked on all fours. Its legs were sturdy, and it had large thumb spikes. Like all **sauropods** it was a herbivore and would have eaten vast amounts of plant matter each day to fuel its large mass.

Vulcanodon lived about **180 million years ago**. Its fossil remains were found in Zimbabwe, southern Africa. Its estimated length was 20 feet (6.1 m) and it weighed around 4 to 5 tons (3.6–4.5 tonnes).

ZUPAYSAURUS

Zupaysaurus means "devil lizard." In Quechuan (the language of the people from the central Andes of South America) "zupay" means devil. It was a carnivorous **theropod**, with muscular legs to run down its prey. It was a large **theropod** for its time and had an unusual head crest similar to *Dilophosaurus* (see page 11). It had slightly elongated vertebrae, which suggests it had a long neck and tail.

Zupaysaurus lived **208–199 million years ago**. Its fossil remains were found in Argentina, South America. It grew to between 13 and 18 feet (4–5.5 m) long and weighed around 440 pounds (200 kg).

ankylosaur
A family of bulky quadrupedal, armored dinosaurs that had a club-like tail. The family included *Ankylosaurus* and *Euoplocephalus*.

ceratosaur
A member of a group of theropod dinosaurs sharing an ancestry with *Ceratosaurus*.

cetiosaur
A member of a family of sauropods.

coelophysid
A family of primitive carnivorous theropod dinosaurs that flourished in the Upper Triassic and Lower Jurassic periods.

dinosauriform
A group of reptiles that include the dinosaurs and their most immediate relatives.

ichthyosaur
A member of the group of large marine reptiles that looked similar to today's dolphins.

massospondylid
A member of a family of sauropodomorphs that existed in Asia, Africa and South America.

ornithischian
A group of dinosaurs characterized by their "bird-hips" and beaks.

plesiosaur
A group of marine reptiles that thrived in the Jurassic and Cretaceous periods, so successful that they had a worldwide oceanic distribution.

pterosaur
Flying reptile group that includes Pterodactylus.

sauropod
A group of large, four-legged, herbivorous dinosaurs with long necks and long tails. This group included the well-known *Brachiosaurus*, *Diplodocus* and *Apatosaurus*.

sauropodomorph
A member of the long-necked, herbivorous dinosaurs that includes the sauropods and their ancestral relatives.

therapsid
A member of a group of animals that includes mammals and their ancestors, whose legs stand more vertically beneath their bodies than is usual in reptiles.

theropod
The large group of lizard-hipped dinosaurs that walked on two legs and included most of the giant carnivores such as *Tyrannosaurus*.

INDEX